Praise for *Bur*

"This is a book that must be savoi...
spaces. The poems in this evocative collection live, dance,
dream, re-create the sounds of rain, the nostalgia of the Cuban
diaspora, the faith in a homeland. You will be touched by their
haunting sensibilities, by their contradictions, but mostly by
their humanity."

— Marjorie Agosín

"*Burnt Sugar* brings together a good number of essential Cuban
poets. The collection can itself be read like one long, intense
poem. Its unity comes from that particular way in which every
Cuban looks back and recognizes each other in a gesture, in a
word, in a kind of nostalgia that is vast and sunlit like a beauti-
ful homeland."

— Mayra Montero,
author of *Captain of the Sleepers*

"These poems have taken me through a *viaje* — through verdant
gardens of exotic flora, on ships that travel through Cuba's
many rivers, and always to the strains of the bittersweet
melodies which absence and distance will painfully recall. Envi
sioning Cuba through the eyes and souls of these poets has been
a unique experience and a rare opportunity to gain insight into
their reality."

— Eva de la O,
executive director, Música de Cámara

"Cubans need poetry, just as we need music. Rhythm is all
around us, from the sway of a woman's hips when she walks to
the rustling of palm fronds in the wind. Our collective heart

pulses to the melodic cadence of words. This bittersweet collection is a mirror reflecting the joy and pathos of being Cuban. While Hijuelos's own Cuban longings give structure and meaning to the selection, Carlson, a poet in her own right, brings the musical lifeblood of Cuba to her sensual, radiant translations."

—Maricel E. Presilla,
culinary historian and restaurateur

*f*P

CONTEMPORARY CUBAN POETRY IN ENGLISH AND SPANISH

BURNT SUGAR

CAÑA QUEMADA

Edited by **LORI MARIE CARLSON**
and **OSCAR HIJUELOS**

with an introduction by **OSCAR HIJUELOS**

FREE PRESS
New York   London   Toronto   Sydney

FREE PRESS
A Division of Simon & Schuster, Inc.
1230 Avenue of the Americas
New York, NY 10020

First Free Press trade paperback edition 2006

FREE PRESS and colophon are trademarks of Simon & Schuster, Inc.

For information regarding special discounts for bulk purchases,
please contact Simon & Schuster Special Sales at 1-800-456-6798
or business@simonandschuster.com

Permissions acknowledgments start on page 115.

Manufactured in the United States of America

10 9 8 7 6 5 4 3 2 1

Library of Congress Cataloging-in-Publication Data
Burnt sugar / caña quemada : contemporary Cuban poetry :
in English and Spanish / edited by Lori Marie Carlson
and Oscar Hijuelos ; with an introduction by Oscar Hijuelos
p. cm.
1. Cuban poetry-Translations into English. 2. Cuban poetry-20th century.
I. Carlson, Lori M. II. Hijuelos, Oscar. III. Title.
PQ7383.5.E5 B87 2006
861'.608097291-dc22   2005058027

ISBN-13: 978-0-7432-7662-7
ISBN-10: 0-7432-7662-0

In memory of
August Wilson,
and to
Constanza Romero,
with our abiding love

Contents

Editors' Note

Although most Americans are aware that Cuban culture has music at its core, less known is that Cuba has always been a nation of poets. Its greatest hero, an icon to Cubans everywhere, is the poet José Martí, but there have been numerous others — from Plácido to José Lezama Lima. Yet the passion for poetry is so strongly rooted in the verbal tradition that writing verse is a common pastime for ordinary folks as well.

The playfulness and vivacity of the Cuban vernacular is as raucous as any mambo. It is informed by a vital mix of African slang — wordplay, religious and cultural imagery — and it flies nearly effortlessly from many a mouth, remaining a culturally defining quality. Influenced by the Yoruba language, *cubanismos* — colorful linguistic expressions — make Spanish spoken by Cubans a musical form all its own and imbue daily life with a wisdom rarely found in English. Beauty and beat permeate the conversations of Cubans, and a kind of sweetness of disposition is part of that lyricism.

In creating this book of twentieth-century poetry written by Cubans of four generations, we hope to convey to an American audience something of the very particular life experiences of those who share Cuban heritage. This is not a volume that offers a survey of Cuban poetry but rather an intimate collection, meant to inspire further reading.

In our original concept for this eclectic sampling of twentieth-century Cuban verse, we had sought to include insightful examples of this art as practiced by poets whose works celebrate their essential "Cubanness" or "Cubanía," regardless of their locality. We had selected poems that reflect a state of mind, an essence formed by the psychological and emotional legacy that all Cubans, whether living here in the United States, in Cuba, or elsewhere, share: the poignancy of being Cuban, their common touchstone.

Though we had been guided by the principle that poetry, coming as it does from the heart and soul of its creators, should be thought to transcend politics, we had proceeded with the notion of including current poetry from Cuba (and poetry by some of the masters of the genre who are no longer living but whose heirs live in Cuba) as a means to convey a realistic and more complete portrait of Cuban poetic activity in our time. However, current U.S. regulations, set forth by the Department of Treasury, rendered it too uncomfortable—both from a practical as well as a legal standpoint—to do so. In the end we had to regretfully eliminate these poets from *Burnt Sugar*.

Still, this collection remains a valuable sampling of the Cuban poetic voice as it exists and thrives today. Even if space did not permit us to incorporate works by many a fine poet of Cuban heritage, what poems we did include were selected on the basis of aesthetic compatibility. In the way that a fine chorus is created, we have tried to bring together beautiful examples of voice—one poem per poet—that work well together as a whole harmonically, and convey the vibrant music and vivid imagery that is uniquely Cuban. These poems are about the glory of nature, the healing power of erotic love, the universality of the human condition, and the mystery of religious faith.

With four exceptions—"Elegía de María Belén Chacón" by Emilio Ballagas, "Sugarcane" by Achy Obejas, "To the Rumba Players of Belén, Cuba . . . An Interpretation of a Song" by Adrián Castro, and "Secretos" by Lissette Méndez— the poems are presented bilingually. "Elegía de María Belén

Chacón" quite simply presents language so unyielding to translation that it remains in its originality, alone. And Adrián Castro's, Achy Obejas's, and Lissette Méndez's poems are firmly rooted in their hybrid use of both English and Spanish.

Above all, while forgiving this collection's lamentable exclusions, think of it as an immersion into an endlessly rich and varied artistic form that flows like a river without beginning or end, or as Eugenio Florit so masterfully says in his poem "Memories," like "the blood of [a] native land."

March 2006

Introduction

Oscar Hijuelos

As I write this introduction to *Burnt Sugar,* I do so with a very strong memory of how my late mother, Magdalena Torrens Hijuelos—a native of Holguín, Cuba, who'd come to the United States in the 1940s—did not for one second of her sixty years in this country ever forget, not even for a single day, what she called "la gloria y belleza de Cuba." To commemorate this, for as long as I can remember she resorted to the practice, so common to Cubans, of writing poems. Hers were sometimes simple pictures of incidents she remembered from her youth; a portrait, circa 1928, of some vain dandy, dressed entirely in white, with a crush on her who might be strolling by her house with a bouquet of carnations—"ese fulano, vestido en blanco, con una vanidad profunda"; the feeling that came over her when the sunlit afternoons, moving ever so slowly and tranquilly, were suddenly disrupted by a sudden fierce downpour, "un aguacero de Dios." She loved birds, *los pajaritos,* that sang in her garden, and often compared herself and her female companions to them, fluttering along in life, coquettishly. Angels and flowers were rife in her poems as well. One of them went:

> Este es mi libro
> Este es mi sueño
> Esta es la flor
> Que perfume mi alrededor

Este es el niño
Que llora porque
Sueña está perdido
Este es el agua
Que corre sin
Saber que es un río
Este es mi corazón
Que gime y
Ríe a la vez
Porque fue martirizado
Hoy no sufro
No padezco
Sólo confío en Dios

This is my book
This is my dream
This is the flower
that perfumes my room
This is the boy
who weeps
because he dreams he is lost
This is the water
that flows without knowing
it is a river
This is my heart that laughs and moans
Because He was martyred
I do not suffer
nor do I want
I trust only in God

Whether her poems were great or accomplished did not seem to matter to her, as she took much pride in the natural, albeit unschooled, artistry she attached to them. Hearing so much about Cuba, of her own Catalan roots (my grandfather had come to Cuba before the turn of the century), and of the Catholicism and more animistic and magical Afro-Cuban beliefs that she had been raised with, I always felt that her visions of a remembered Cuba were being filtered through some poetic mesh, for nothing she wrote about was ever just what it seemed to be.

And I got the feeling that she wrote out of pure necessity, because in her day, what existed of Cuba in this country, aside from the mambo of the 1950s and such small pockets of Cuban-Anglo common ground as *I Love Lucy*, resided in the anecdotes and songs of Cubans themselves. I suppose that if she, as an immigrant who took too many years to learn English, had been associated with a university, she might have well immersed herself in the grand legacy of Cuban poetry, but this was not possible for her in her time. As a little girl she had learned some of José Martí's more patriotic verses, but mainly her poems were influenced by the cadences of prayer and of heart-felt boleros. She lived long enough to see the popular cultural scene in this country change, many of her evenings spent watching the Telemundo and Univisión Spanish-language networks with their *telenovelas* and variety shows; and though she had often haunted many a bookshop in the neighborhood she lived in, as much as she looked and looked, I doubt if she ever thought to find any books relating to the poetic side of Cuba, in the way she understood it—as being something neither lofty nor overly erudite, but capturing the voices that were of "los cubanos," such as she encountered in her everyday life.

Like so many Cubans in this country, she, politically speaking, had never been enamored of the Cuban revolution, which had, in effect, shut her off forever from her homeland (nor did she forget her own family's difficulties in that period). But when she spoke of the Cubans on the island, she never did so with severity; they were "los pobrecitos"—"the poor ones"—

who had been overwhelmed by historical circumstances. Castro, and any form of tyranny, she abhorred, but never had she shown any malice to "her people."

So I like to think of this anthology as something she would have much enjoyed, for it is not about politics, but about voices, other Cuban voices different from her own, but each representing a different aspect of the "diaspora" that we Cubans, born here or there, represent. This is the kind of book that would have surely amazed her.

BURNT SUGAR

CAÑA QUEMADA

The Rain

Gustavo Pérez Firmat

I miss the rain.
Tonight when it finally pours again
I know the rain
surrounds the house and makes it safe.
(Thanks to the rain once more we'll be an island.)

Tonight I know that true paradise
was not the Garden but the Ark.
Noah with his brood and beasts
asleep on planks:
skin against skin, mouth to mouth
one contiguous heart.

Tonight I know
there is no greater good than intimacy
no finer luxury than isolation.

I hope it rains until the end of the world
so that no one ever leaves my house.
Children, anchor yourselves to me
this storm will last awhile.

tr. from the Spanish by Lori M. Carlson

La lluvia

Gustavo Pérez Firmat

Extraño la lluvia.
Esta noche que por fin vuelve a cántaros
sé que la lluvia
ciñe la casa y la protege.
(Por la lluvia volvemos a ser isla).

Esta noche sé que el auténtico paraíso
no fue el Jardín sino el Arca:
Noé con vástagos y criaturas
dormidos entre tablas:
piel con piel, boca con boca,
y el corazón contiguo.

Esta noche sé
que no hay mayor bien que la intimidad
ni mayor lujo que el aislamiento.

Por eso quiero que llueva hasta el fin del mundo
para que nadie nunca deje mi casa.
Hijos, ánclense a mí,
hay tormenta para rato.

Rain

José Abreu Felippe

Everything has overflowed
as if existence in the air were
a silent downpour,
this softening of walls
that everything descends, washes away
or transfigures.
Days do come, however, and the air,
color, life take hold in me
gushing in desire to keep going.

tr. from the Spanish by Lori M. Carlson

Lluvia

José Abreu Felippe

Todo se ha derramado
como si en el aire la existencia fuera
ese gotear silencioso,
este reblandecimiento de las paredes
que todo lo desciende, lo despoja,
lo transfigura.
Sin embargo los días se suceden y el aire,
el color, la vida, se adentran en mí
y hacen brotar deseos de seguir.

1898 Vistas

Enrique Sacerio-Garí

The Eve of San Juan has a magic eye on the water . . .

Who is to say
what our grandmothers were doing in 1898:
gazing over a burning harbor or a casualty list,
hugging a wounded sailor at the water's edge,
a blue jacket stained with blood and coal dust from the *Maine*,
or crying for the mambises in Matanzas
and for Calixto García's own tears
as he waited outside Santiago
while the Americans marched into the city with their flag . . . ?

Who is to say
if our grandmothers sat on soft cushions and wore jewels
of red and green glittering in the brightest chambers
or if dark skin glowing red,
facing a charcoal maker's heap,

a girl heard bullets approaching from both sides . . . ?
Who is to say whose son ran up a hurtful hill
or whose child touched Clara Barton's hand
or how Clara Maass died in Las Animas
or why only Jefferson University honors Carlos Finlay . . . ?

Headlines claimed Cuba Libre
(and Daiquirí: the site of the landing)
against a proud machete resistance,
raising the cannons of the strongest ships
(and glasses to toast the new empire . . .)

Summer nights clear the memories
but our political storms replay the oldest wars . . .

Who is to say
what our grandmothers were doing in 1898,
who can see what shaped the contour of their hands:
a fine glass? a diamond? or the darkest hour
of the charcoal makers?

tr. from the Spanish by the author

Vistas del 1898

Enrique Sacerio-Garí

La víspera de San Juan guarda un ojo mágico en el agua...

¿Quién nos va a decir
lo que hacían nuestras abuelas en 1898:
se asomaban por ver un puerto ardiendo o una lista de bajas,
por abrazar a un marinero herido al borde del agua
uniformes azules manchados de sangre y polvo de carbón del
       Maine,
o lloraban por los mambises de Matanzas
y por las lágrimas de Calixto García
que esperaba en las afueras de Santiago
mientras los americanos marchaban a la ciudad con su bandera...?

¿Quién nos va a decir
si nuestras abuelas se sentaban en cómodos cojines y llevaban
joyas rojas y verdes resplandecientes en las cámaras más iluminadas
o si piel oscura colorada incandescente,
ante la lomita del carbonero

una niña oyó las balas acercándose de ambos lados...?
¿Quién nos va a decir de quién era el hijo que subió la loma dolorosa
o de quién era el hijo que tocó la mano de Clara Barton
o como murió Clara Maass en Las Animas
o por qué sólo la Universidad de Jefferson honra a Carlos
       Finlay...?

Los titulares declaraban Cuba Libre
(y Daiquirí: donde desembarcaron)
contra la orgullosa resistencia del machete,

alzando los cañones de los buques más fuertes
(y las copas para brindar por el nuevo imperio...)
Las noches de verano aclaran la memoria
pero nuestras tormentas políticas recurvan las guerras más antiguas...

¿Quién nos va a decir
lo que hacían nuestras abuelas en 1898,
quién logra ver lo que conforma sus manos:
una copa de cristal fino, un diamante
o la hora más oscura de los carboneros?

Autumn Presents Me with a Leaf

Reinaldo Arenas

Autumn presents me with a leaf.
Trembling like a supplicant, I imagine,
it's just fallen beside me.
Final flame dissolving,
a leaf demands my closest attention,
my most generous devotion.

Autumn presents me with a leaf.
Remote fragrance, final blush,
its only branch is the unlikely gaze of a passerby,
its only salvation is my farewell.

                              A leaf,
in desperation, tries to lodge itself in my breast.
It wants the gentle greeting of the vagabond,
the fraternal gaze of the condemned man,
the warm complicity of the curse.
But what can I do with it
if my reckless life of a visiting professor
barely allows me to collect textbooks?

Indifferent to my justifications,
frail and stubborn as hope,
it asks to be sheltered by my fingers.
But what can I do with this specter
that pales before me, detached from the vital tree?
On the other hand,
I'm a specialist in nineteenth-century Cuban literature.
I know nothing about botany.

Autumn presents me with a leaf
that without much fanfare takes hold of me,
and turned into a sheet of paper,
compels me to draw on it my self-portrait.

Autumn presents me with a leaf
—a blank sheet of paper—
infinite homeland of the exile
where all the furies whirl.

Autumn presents me with a leaf.

(Ithaca, October 1985)

tr. from the Spanish by Daniel Shapiro

El otoño me regala una hoja

Reinaldo Arenas

El otoño me regala una hoja.
Con temblor que imagino suplicante
acaba de caer junto a mí.
Ultima llama que se disuelve,
una hoja reclama mi atención más exacta,
mi más desprendida devoción.

El otoño me regala una hoja.
Remota fragrancia, final rubor,
no tiene otra rama que la improbable mirada de un transeúnte,
no cuenta con otra salvación que mi despedida.

                                 Una hoja
desesperadamente pretende instalarse en mi pecho.
Quiere el leve saludo del vagabundo,
la hermana mirada del condenado,
la cálida complicidad de la maldición.
Pero ¿qué puedo hacer con ella
si mi temeraria vida de profesor visitante
apenas se me permite coleccionar libros de texto?

Indiferente a mis justificaciones,
frágil y terca como la esperanza,
pide ser acogida por mis dedos.
Pero ¿qué puedo hacer con este espectro
que ante mí empalidece desprendido del árbol vital?
Por otra parte
yo me especializo en literatura cubana del siglo 19.
Nada sé de botánica.

El otoño me regala una hoja
que sin mayores trámites se apodera de mí
y convertida ya en hoja de papel
me obliga a dibujar en ella mi autorretrato.

El otoño me regala una hoja
—una hoja blanca de papel—,
patria infinita del desterrado
donde todas las furias se arremolinan.

El otoño me regala una hoja.

(Ithaca, octubre de 1985)

I Have Always Lived in Cuba

Heberto Padilla

I live in Cuba.
I have always lived in Cuba.
Those years of roaming the world,
of which much has been said,
are my lies, my falsehoods.

As I have always been in Cuba.

And it is true
that there were days of the Revolution
when the island
could blow apart in the waves;
but in the airports
in the places where I traveled
I felt
that they screamed at me
              by name
and responding
I was on this shore
sweating,
      walking,
             in shirtsleeves,
drunk
      on wind and greenery
when sun and sea bathe the terraces
  and sing their alleluia.

tr. from the Spanish by Lori M. Carlson

Siempre he vivido en Cuba

Heberto Padilla

Yo vivo en Cuba.
Siempre he vivido en Cuba.
Esos años de vagar por el mundo,
de que tanto han hablado,
son mis mentiras, mis falsificaciones.

Porque yo siempre he estado en Cuba.

Y es cierto
que hubo días de la Revolución
en que la Isla
pudo estallar entre las olas;
pero en los aeropuertos,
en los sitios que anduve
sentí
que me gritaban
              por mi nombre
y al responder
yo estaba en esta orilla
sudando,
            andando,
                    en mangas de camisa,
borracho
            de viento y de follaje
cuando el sol y el mar trepan a las terrazas
   y cantan su aleluya.

A Poem for the Epiphany

Pablo Medina

for Ellen Jacko

It snows because the door to heaven is open,
because God is tired of working
and the day needs to be left alone.
It snows because there is a widow hiding
under her mother's bed,
because the birds are resting their throats
and three wise men are offering gifts.
Because the clouds are singing
and trees have a right to exist,
because the horses of the past are returning.
They are gray and trot gently into the barn
never touching the ground.

It snows because the wind wants
to be water, because water
wants to be powder and powder wants
to seduce the eye. Because once in his life
the philosopher has to admit
to the poverty of thought.
Because the rich man cannot buy snow
and the poor man has to wear it on his eyebrows.
Because it makes the old dog think
his life has just begun. He runs
back and forth across the parking lot.
He rolls on the snow. He laps it up.

It snows because light and dark
are making love in a field where old age
has no meaning, where colors blur,
silence covers sound, sleep covers sorrow,
everything is death, everything is joy.

Poema de la epifanía

Pablo Medina

Para Ellen Jacko

Nieva porque la puerta del cielo se abre,
porque Dios se cansa de trabajar
y el día requiere tranquilidad.
Nieva porque una viuda se esconde
bajo el lecho de su madre,
tres reyes magos hacen ofrendas
y las aves descansan la voz.

Nieva para que las nubes canten
y los árboles afirmen su derecho a existir.
Los potros del pasado regresan.
Son grises y entran al establo dócilmente
trotando sin pisar el andén.

Nieva porque el viento quiere ser agua,
el agua quiere ser polvo y el polvo
quiere seducir la vista. Porque alguna vez
el filósofo tiene que admitir
la pobreza de su pensar.
El rico no puede comprar la nieve
y el pobre tiene que llevarla en su mirar.
Porque la nieve convence al perro viejo
que su vida acaba de comenzar.
Corre de un lado a otro del parqueo,
se revuelca en la nieve, la quiere mordisquear.

Nieva porque la luz y la oscuridad
hacen el amor en un campo
donde la vejez no tiene sentido,
los colores se mezclan,
el silencio abraza el sonido,
el sueño abraza el dolor,
luego todo es muerte, todo es felicidad.

tr. del inglés por el autor

I've Never Seen It Snow

Agustín Acosta

Love, I've never seen it snow. My poor peaks
love the sun. They are ignorant of frost and cold.
The blue sky makes a magic roof
and winters are translucent, brief.

I am a child of the tropics, and all my visions
are of clear auroras, glittering sunsets.
My chain of dreams has no more links
and now I know my path's direction.

I ignored your love of snowcaps,
somber hours, withered roses,
and in a flickering night among the shadows I saw you,

apart from the sweet brilliance of my moonlight.
And upon you, a mountain yourself, dream-made, a
cosmic indifference snowed.

tr. from the Spanish by Lori M. Carlson

Yo nunca he visto nevar

Agustín Acosta

Amor, yo nunca he visto nevar. Mis pobres cumbres
aman el sol. Ignoran los fríos y nieves.
El cielo azul fabrica sus mágicas techumbres
y sus inviernos son traslúcidos y breves.

Yo soy el hijo del trópico, y todas mis visiones
son las claras auroras y fúlgidos ocasos.
Mi cadena de sueños ya no tiene eslabones,
y ya sé hacia qué rumbo se dirigen mis pasos.

Yo ignoraba tu amor por las cumbres nevadas,
por las horas sombrías, por las rosas ajadas,
y en una noche trémula entre sombras te vi,

ajena al dulce brillo de mi claro de luna.
Y, montaña tú misma, hecha de sueño, una
indiferencia cósmica nevaba sobre ti.

From Head to Toe
(allegro giocoso)

Luis Cartañá

We did it in the kitchen among pots
full of roaches;
we did it as we turned the corner of a street,
lying on the carpet in your room
looking out the window at a rainbow maybe;

we did it absent Lorca's moon

to the clamor of a country fair,
sitting on the toilet, in the tub, so happy
on top of your felt bear
shaking loose the dust,

in candlelight
so happy!

oh, woman after giving birth
three times nearly, virgin like the navel
of the Virgin;

we did it looking north
on your aunt's precious cushions
and patriotically,

behind the back of your blind grandma,
we did it falling into rapture
letting go the one thing that we owned,

a bridge across an empty riverbed
we did it;

we did it reacquainting ourselves
in time with utmost excitement
quiet

we did it among your cats
pouncing lightly on our bodies
with eyes surprised

we did it climbing the stairs
from the first step to the last;
we did it every way imaginable
we did it asking the question,
we did it sad almost laughing
with joy; we did it happy almost crying
with grief; we did it as if saying hi
as if saying goodbye.

tr. from the Spanish by Lori M. Carlson

Desde tus ojos a tus piernas
(allegro giocoso)

Luis Cartañá

Lo hicimos en la cocina entre calderos
repletos de cucarachas;
lo hicimos al doblar de cualquier esquina,
en los rincones de tu habitación sobre las alfombras,
mirando afuera de la ventana quizá un arco iris;

lo hicimos sin la luna de Lorca,

entre la algarabía de la feria del pueblo,
encima del inodoro, en la bañera, ¡ay alegres!
sobre el oso de peluche
soltando el aserrín,

bajo la luz de una vela
¡ay, alegres!

ay doncella despues de parir
casi tres hijos, virgen como el ombligo
de la Virgen;

lo hicimos mirando al norte,
sobre las sagradas almohadas de tu tía
y arropados en la bandera,

en las narices de tu abuela la ciega,
lo hicimos como cayéndose en la nada
y sujetando lo único que poseíamos,

como un puente que salta un río seco
lo hicimos;

lo hicimos como reconociéndonos
a tiempo la última alegría
que callamos;

lo hicimos entre tus gatos
caminando sobre nuestros cuerpos
con ojos sorprendidos,

lo hicimos subiendo las escaleras
desde el primer al último escalón;
lo hicimos por todo lo hacible
del cuerpo; lo hicimos haciéndonos la pregunta;
lo hicimos tristes casi riendo
de alegría; lo hicimos alegres casi llorando
de tristeza; lo hicimos como saludándonos
o diciéndonos adiós.

Feet

Rafael Catalá

responsible are feet that walk knowingly
on tiled floors

loving are feet in their rhythm caressing
earth

erudite are feet on the path and
embankment and sand

erotic are feet in shoes and shoeless
under sheets rubbing against my thighs

tr. from the Spanish by Lori M. Carlson

Los pies

Rafael Catalá

responsables los pies que saben caminar
sobre ladrillos

amantes los pies en su ritmo acariciante
hacia la tierra

eruditos los pies en la carrera y salto
en terraplén y arena

eróticos los pies en los zapatos, y fuera
en la sábana rozándome los muslos

Loving You Is a Way of Being

Angel Cuadra

Loving you is a way of being.
I watch the years pass like the smoke
that goes rising in blues, and is lost.
Life has an identical profile
that reappears sometimes, and is its constant always.
I have the profile of loving you forever.
I have assumed that gesture from the beginning.
It seems that I have come to this corner of the world
to tell the universe I love you.
Occasionally the world exists to contain us:
a transient vessel that holds
our contents.

It is a way of being: loving you is that.
An attitude toward life;
almost a life in itself, an absolute.
A circle, of which each point is the end
and each point the beginning.

The plenitude of being rests in your embrace,
like coming close to quiet.
And being quiet is your way.

Complete am I only when I love you.

tr. from the Spanish by Lori M. Carlson

Amarte es un modo de ser

Angel Cuadra

Amarte es un modo de ser.
Miro pasar los años como el humo
que va subiendo azules, y se pierde.
La vida tiene un perfil idéntico
que reaparece a veces, y es su constante siempre.
Tengo el perfil de amarte desde siempre.
He adaptado ese gesto, creo que desde antes.
Parece que he venido a esta esquina del mundo
para decirle al mundo que te quiero.
El mundo sirve, a veces, para contenernos:
vaso de tránsito que tiene
en este punto el contenido nuestro.

Es un modo de ser: amarte es eso.
Una actitud ante la vida;
casi una vida en sí, como absoluto.
Círculo es, que en cada punto es fin
y en cada punto inicio.

La plenitud del ser está en tu abrazo,
como el acercamiento a lo inaudito.
Y es lo inaudito la costumbre
de ti.

Yo sólo soy total cuando te quiero.

Memories

Eugenio Florit

The soul gets into the habit of its dreams,
and rests there, quietly.
But there are times, like this afternoon,
when the sky, a color, some pigeons
make us ponder far-off things;
on what kept us going under the sun.
(Or was it last night's music, or the words
we spoke at lunch,
as when discussing the past, we felt
the slightest tug of absence . . .)
Fine. But fact is we do remember.
Memory comes with light, a perfume
and we feel something
like river water coming toward us
submerging our hearts
in pleasant shadows, green coolness;
oh, and the mind wants to go back
and gaze upon its mountains and seas
promising itself to see what it hasn't seen
and ask the earth for forgiveness,
for not gazing more kindly upon it at the time.
Now the man thinks back to the day
when as a child he cried, disillusioned
by the fountain of his dreams that was just
a simple droplet
turned waterspout by his imagination.

Now the rivers rush forth.
The Cuyaguateje is passing with its history

and the Ariguanabo, so loved by my grandparents;
the Almendares emptying into the seas
amid the hustle and bustle of bridges and steel,
and leaving behind it, like a memory,
a solitary palm on its banks;
and the Habanilla flows
surging over its rocks;
and earlier, the San Juan and Yumurí Rivers
—whose names alone could weave a legend—;
and the Tuinucú rushes by in birdsong,
and finally the splendid Cauto River arrives
born and raised in the Sierra Maestra
before it dies in the Caribbean Sea
in the arms of its sparkling waves.

Lord, let me be aware of all my rivers,
the ones I know, the ones I should know;
because to know rivers
is to know the land through which they flow;
because to know rivers
is to know the trees they reflect,
the stones which kiss them,
the birds nesting on their shores
and the fish darting through their waters.
To know rivers
is to know the blood of your native land.

tr. from the Spanish by David Unger

Recuerdos

Eugenio Florit

El alma se acostumbra con su sueño,
y en él se está, callada.
Pero hay horas, así, como esta tarde,
en que un cielo, un color, unas palomas
nos llevan a pensar en lo distante;
en lo que, bajo el sol, nos mantenía.
(O fue la música de anoche, o las palabras
que en el almuerzo pronunciamos,
cuando, a hablar de ayer, sentimos
un pequeño dolor de ausencia...)
Bien. Pero el caso es que recordamos.
Que en el recuerdo vienen luz, perfume,
y que sentimos algo
como un agua de río que nos llega
y nos inunda el corazón
de sombra grata, de frescura verde;
ay, y quiere volver el pensamiento
a mirar sus montañas y sus mares
y se promete ver lo que no ha visto,
y le pide perdones a la tierra,
porque en su tiempo no la vio mejor.
Ahora piensa el hombre en aquel día
en que, aún niño, lloró de desencanto
por la fuente en los sueños, que no era
más que una humilde gota de agua
hecha, en su fantasía, surtidor.

Ahora vienen los ríos.
Pasa el Cuyaguateje con su historia

y Ariguanabo, amor de mis abuelos;
pasa Almendares dándose a las olas
entre un trajín de puentes y de hierros
y dejándose atrás, para recuerdo,
la solitaria palma en sus orillas;
pasa el Hanabanilla
que salta entre sus rocas;
y aún antes, el San Juan y el Yumurí
—nombres los dos para tejer leyenda—;
y pasa el Tuinucú con sonido de pájaro,
y llega al fin el Cauto espléndido
que en la Sierra Maestra nace y crece,
y va a morir en donde el mar Caribe
con sus olas de luces lo recibe.

Señor, dame saber todos mis ríos,
los que conozco ya, los que me faltan;
porque saber los ríos
es saberse la tierra por que pasan;
porque saber los ríos
es conocer el árbol que retratan,
es conocer las piedras que los besan,
los pájaros que anidan en su orilla
y los peces que juegan en sus aguas.
Que saberse los ríos
es conocer la sangre de la patria.

Weariness

Orlando Rossardi

This afternoon that slams in my way I'm tired of virtually
    everything
I'm tired of water, of stones, of making do and distance;
of the I that ages among no one, of time that discovers
    its parts,
of solitude that explodes in emptiness, of purity that doesn't
    count,
of you so carefully guarded and lashing on the banks like a
    bridge.
I'm tired of absence, and also of sameness.
And this afternoon, suddenly, I'm tired of grace
and disgrace, of command and countermand of suffering
and being by virtue of happiness tender and useless as a peach.
I'm tired of this useless, blank page,
of regret and laughter, of siege and condemnation;
of being, and of suddenly being sunk in tinder;
of hunger and of conscience I'm tired, of air that gives rise
to the voice of hands fashioning, tirelessly, words.
I'm tired—to the brim of the perfume of rain,
of God being a pretext for catastrophes, of
rotting away walking the hallways and offices, of thinking
    deeply
about life and survival, of drinking with my eyes from empty
    vessels,
of livid lips like wounds and the smell of uninhabited skin.
From the very depths of my being I'm tired; from A to Z,
from my head to my toes, with its periods and commas,
just as Neruda was tired, the way that Vallejo cracked up,
just as Blas Otero was fed up with death, the way Celaya

suddenly burst up to bury his land. This afternoon I'm tired
    of everything, abysmally, and so it's not so strange
I settle down in murmurs—don't scream, don't make noise—
    and
let begin and leave alone, like this afternoon is passing, this
    poem.

tr. from the Spanish by Lori M. Carlson

Cansancio

Orlando Rossardi

Esta tarde que pega en mi camino me he cansado de todo,
    virtualmente
Me he cansado del agua, de las piedras, del hacer y la distancia;
del yo que se madura entre ninguno, del tiempo que descubre
    sus fragmentos,
del solo que revienta en su vacío, de lo puro que no importa,
de ti guardada adentro y hostigando en las orillas como un
    puente.
Me he cansado del vocablo ausencia, y también de la
    monotonía.
Y esta tarde, como a golpes, me he cansado de la gracia
y la desgracia, del mando y del desmande, del sufrir
y del estar por mi alegría tierno y desvalido como un
    durazno.
Me he cansado hasta del desplome de esta página vacía,
de la pena y de la risa, del asedio y la condena;
del ser, y estar de pronto como hundido entre la yesca;
del hambre y la conciencia me he cansado, del aire que vocea
el ruido de las manos tallando, incansablemente, las palabras.
Me he cansado —para colmo— del perfume de las lluvias,
de Dios haciendo de pretexto por los golpes, de podrirme
a pierna suelta por pasillos y oficinas, de pensar en serio
en vida y sobrevida, de beber de ojos y vasijas huecas,
de labios vivos como una herida y del olor a piel
    deshabitada.
¡Desde el fondo de mi mismo me he cansado; de la A a la Z,
de los pies a la cabeza, con sus puntos y sus comas,
como se cansó también Neruda, del modo que estalló Vallejo,
que fue hartándose de muerte Blas de Otero, que Celaya

prorrumpió de golpe hasta entrañar su tierra! Esta tarde
me he cansado de todo, abismalmente, y no es raro que me
        albergue
en los susurros—que no grite ni haga ruidos—que empiece
y luego deje por cansancio, como esta tarde va pasando, este
        poema.

To José Martí

Walter de las Casas

freedom, more freedom
one hundred years pass
and I have witnessed
the new homage to
yes, dear José,
that which results more by conquering
not singing

tr. from the Spanish by Lori M. Carlson

A José Martí

Walter de las Casas

libertad, más libertad
cien años pasan
y yo he presenciado
el nuevo homenaje
a lo que
sí, querido José,
menos se debe cantar
que conquistar

Obatalá

Severo Sarduy

White garments if you pray to him.
Sixteen parrot feathers.
Snake, ivory—and never gold—
for the lord of heads.
With his cane he minds you.
Careful that he doesn't take revenge
should he see carousing, revelry, or orgy.
Cascarilla, cotton, cream
offer him with bits of silver
and a tower of meringue.

tr. from the Spanish by Lori M. Carlson

Obatalá

Severo Sarduy

Ropa blanca si le rezas.
Dieciséis plumas de loro.
Majá, marfil —y nunca oro—
al dueño de las cabezas.
Con su bastón te enderezas.
Cuida de que no se vengue
si ve juerga, orgía o jelengue.
Cascarilla, algodón, nata,
dale con grajeas de plata
y una torre de merengue.

Song to the Sugarcane

Virgil Suárez

At Publix today with my daughters
I spotted the green stalks of sugarcane,

tucked under the boxed Holland tomatoes,
ninety-eight cents a stalk. I grabbed the three

left and brought them home. My daughters,
born in the United States, unlike me, stand

in the kitchen in awe as I take the serrated
knife and peel away the hard green layer

exposing the fibrous white, pure slices.
"Here," I say, "nothing is ever as sweet as this."

We stand in the kitchen and chew slices
of sugarcane as I tell them this was my candy

when I was a kid growing up in Havana,
this was the only constant sweetness

in my childhood. This delicious, sweet stalk.
You chew on a piece to remember how

to love what you can't have all the time.

Canción a la caña verde

Virgil Suárez

En Publix con mis hijas hoy
vi la caña verde

bajo una caja de tomates holandeses,
noventa y ocho centavos la caña. Compré tres

y las traje a casa. Mis hijas,
nacidas en los Estados Unidos, como yo nunca lo fui, esperan

en la cocina hipnotizadas mientras yo corto un trozo
con un cuchillo, pelando la cascara verde,

a puros pedacitos, lo fibroso una sonrisa blanca.
"Tengan," digo yo, "nunca probarán algo más dulce..."

Parados en la cocina comiendo caña con mis hijas
el caramelo de mi adolescencia

cuando era niño en La Habana
éste era mi dulce constante,

esta deliciosa caña.
Masticas un pedazo para recordarte lo dulce

que es ese amor que no dura toda una vida.

tr. del inglés por el autor

Sugarcane

Achy Obejas

can't cut
cut the cane
azuca' in chicago
dig it down to the
roots sprouting spray paint on the
walls on the hard cold
stone of the great gritty city
slums in chicago
with the mansions in the hole
in the head of
the old rich left behind
from other times lopsided
gangster walls overgrown taken
over by the dark
and poor overgrown with no
sugarcane but you
can't can't cut
cut the water
bro'
from the flow and
you can't can't cut
cut the blood
lines from this island
train one by one throwing off
the chains siguaraya
no no
no se pue'e cortar
pan con ajo quisqueya

cuba y borinquen no
se pue'en parar

I saw it
saw black a-frica
down in the city
walking in chicago y
la cuba cuba
gritando en el solar
I saw it
saw quisqueya
brown
uptown in the city
cryin' in chicago
y borinquen
bor'
sin un
chavo igual but
you can't can't cut
cut the water
bro'
from the flow and
you can't can't cut
cut the blood
lines from this island
train one by one throwing off
the chains siguaraya
no no
no se pue'e cortar
pan con ajo quisqueya
cuba y borinquen no
se pue'en parar

¡azuca'!

Your Darkness, Your Salt

Fayad Jamís

I don't know if it happened yesterday or a long time ago or
    maybe it's happening now
my beast hand, infinitely marine, is writing these words on
    your back
and I feel your mysterious, unfolding flesh, your flesh of the
    earth, your earth crossed
by streams that flow singing from unreachable latitudes

I only know that I have you in hand, that I live tangled in
    your hair,
that at times I barely breathe, I know nothing of the world: I
    don't know if I jump
from my mother's womb or if you give me a kiss and there
    are no windows,
clocks, books, telephones, doors, scissors in this room.

One day you appeared among my things (you came from my
    belongings as if you were one of my boyhood dreams)
and you had that radiant, pure face, guilty of love: you were
    like a doll
about to be transformed into a child or maybe I couldn't
    understand what was happening
and you were already a woman trembling from love and
    eternity in my arms.

Maybe time is turning because I begin to touch your
    presence in my life.
I feel your voice, your darkness, your salt, and I tell you
    again and again that I would be capable

of loving your mouth, loving only your mouth, well no,
          your mouth with your eyes
or even better, all of this that I can't name, take, devour

these groans, these storms of heat, the dark splendor of your
          eyes in shadow,
the total darkness as I, panting, navigating, search for you,
          your body.
You see now what is happening to me: I don't try to
          remember or even less try to tell you that I was
          certain
that the night would rain down stars and melodies on the
          grass of my pillow.

I was accustomed to loveless days, to loves that fill long
          days,
to all the loves that blossom unexpectedly while turning a
          street corner,
to all the loves, almost always glorious, that have spent my
          skeleton
and that, at times, I see shining in a small indistinguishable
          flame in a stranger's eyes.

But you appeared suddenly with incomprehensible doll-like
          gestures
and almost before knowing your name you moved into my
          space.
Now you are part of this vertiginous time of mine sewn with
          nostalgia,
my fingers touch each inch of your skin while you flower in
          my sheets.

Finally I can tell you something that until now was
          impossible: I love this city.

Its streets are now a jungle of lights that, finally, are part of
      your eyes,
that, of course, stop in the waves of your hair or perhaps not,
I barely tell you things that make sense and the only thing I
      know for certain is that I love this city

because I'm loving you, because I feel you as mine until the
      water's depths.
Let this night not end, nor the taste
of your salt in my life. And until the end of time let me tell
stories of a city I loved almost saying good-bye as if saying
      the same to that body

that the universe polished for me and I had a night—
      especially a night—
given to all of my kisses, set inside my space
left forever in one farewell, in a vast, indefinable tenderness.
I know now that all time is the tremor of your salt in my
      life.

tr. from the Spanish by Laura Rocha Nakazawa

Tu oscuridad, tu sal

Fayad Jamís

No sé si ocurrió ayer o fue hace mucho tiempo o tal vez
      sucede en este instante:
mi mano de bestia infinitamente marina escribe estas palabras
      en tu espalda,
y palpo tu carne misteriosa y profunda, tu carne toda tierra,
      tu tierra atravesada
por corrientes de agua que vienen cantando desde
      inalcanzables latitudes.

Sólo sé que te tengo al alcance de mi mano, que vivo
      enredado en tus cabellos,
que a veces casi no respiro ni sé nada del mundo: no sé si salto
desde el vientre de mi madre o es que me das un beso y no
      hay ventanas
ni relojes ni libros ni teléfonos ni puertas ni tijeras en el cuarto.

Un día apareciste entre mis cosas (saliste de mis cosas como
      uno de mis sueños de muchacho)
y ya tenías esa cara radiante y pura y culpable del amor:
      parecías una muñeca
en trance de convertirse en niño o acaso no pude comprender
      lo que pasaba
y ya eras una mujer temblando de amor y eternidad entre mis
      brazos.

Tal vez el tiempo está girando pues empiezo a palpar tu
      presencia en mi vida.
Palpo tu voz, tu oscuridad, tu sal, y te repito tantas veces que
      sería capaz

de amar tu boca, de amar sólo tu boca, o no, tu boca con tus
        ojos,
o, aun mejor, todo esto que no soy capaz de nombrar,
        abarcar, devorar,

estos gemidos, estas tormentas de calor, el brillo oscuro de
        tus ojos en la sombra,
la oscuridad total en que te busco jadeando y navegando por
        tu carne.
Ya ves lo que me pasa: no acierto a recordar y aún menos a
        decirte por qué tenía la certidumbre
de que la noche llovería estrellas y melodías en el pasto de mi
        almohada.

Estaba acostumbrado a días sin amor, a amores que llenan
        largos días,
a todos los amores que nacen inesperadamente al doblar una
        esquina,
a todos los amores, casi siempre gloriosos, que han ido
        gastando mi esqueleto
y que, a veces, veo resplandecer con su pequeña llama
        inextinguible en los ojos de una extraña.

Pero tú apareciste de pronto con incomprensibles gestos de
        muñeca
y casi antes de conocer tu nombre ya te habías instalado en
        mi espacio.
Ya eres parte de este vertiginoso tiempo mío sembrado de
        nostalgia,
mis dedos acarician cada pedazo de tu piel mientras floreces
        en mis sábanas.

Al fin ya puedo decirte algo que hasta hoy fue imposible: que
        amo esta ciudad.

Sus calles son ahora una selva de luces que, desde luego, es
        parte de tus ojos,
que, claro está, terminan en los meandros de tu pelo, o acaso no,
acaso te estoy diciendo palabras sin sentido y lo único cierto
        es que amo esta ciudad

porque te estoy amando, porque te siento mía hasta el fondo
        del agua.
Que no termine nunca esta noche, que no se apague nunca
el sabor de tu sal en mi vida. Y que hasta el fin pueda contar
historias de una ciudad que amé casi al decirle adiós como a
        aquel cuerpo

que el universo pulió para mí y que tuve una noche—sobre
        todo una noche—
entregado a mis besos, incrustado en mi espacio,
quedado para siempre en un adiós, en una enorme ternura
        indefinible.
Ya sé que todo el tiempo es ahora el temblor de tu sal en mi
        vida.

Sleep Apnea

Sandra M. Castillo

Night squeezes an invisible breath
from my chest, a dull, sustained ache
the color of carnival glass,
a dream of an angel at your front door,
his open wings, white and perfect,
guarding your entrances and exits,
un bolero triste con voz de Sandro o Rafael
whispering about seduction
the hand of God
in a world where we take
our clothes off together,
where insanity is a shadow undressing
on the veranda,
a glare of rain in her eyes,
where I wait for you
the way I used to wait
for love.

Apnea

Sandra M. Castillo

La noche me roba un respiro,
una sostenida pena iridiscente,
un sueño de un ángel en tu puerta
sus alas blancas y perfectas
guardando tus entradas y salidas,
un bolero triste con voz de Sandro o Rafael
susurrando sobre la seducción
la mano de Dios
en un mundo donde nos desnudamos juntos,
donde la locura es una sombra
desvistiéndose en la veranda,
un reflejo de lluvia en sus ojos,
donde te espero,
como antes esperaba
el amor.

tr. del inglés por la autora

Secretos

Lissette Méndez

For the third time this week
I return to Corazón's Bodega,
to aisle five's orderly rows of novena candles
plastered with pictures of Catholic saints
better known by their Yoruba names
Ochún, Changó, and Yemayá.

I go back to the carnicero
for cuts of beef with Cuban names
palomilla, picadillo, or costilla de riñonada,
and for jamón serrano I don't eat,
the veins of fat on each slice
thick ripples
I imagine can be deciphered,

just as I yearn
to translate the poetry
of the produce:
frutabombas pregnant with tiny black seeds,
meaty anones,
plátanos verdes
for tostones I show my girlfriend how to make
by cutting the plantain into chunks,
dipping each piece into
the sizzle sizzle of olive oil until lightly
golden, then smashing them,
the fun part,
with my hand fisted or
the little wooden gadget bought on 8th Street,

then back in for a longer sizzle
until golden brown,
crispy cracks on the surface
radiating from the sunny center,
glistening with salt like diamond dust,
another mystery to decipher.

On my fourth return to Corazón's
the butter afternoon sun melting
through the front window
illuminates the stack of latas de frijoles negros con sazón criolla,
creating a glorious halo
around the cashier's homemade blond hair; she's

Nuestra Señora del Bodeguín,

and I want to light a candle to her,
I want her help
finding what I seek
but I don't know
what it is I've lost, so instead
I ask for a loaf of pan cubano,
soft doughy white
like her bosom above
her dulce de guayaba-red
ruffled blouse.

On my fifth visit, for lunch,
I slice open a papa rellena
and scry the insides
like a santera would
the guts of a freshly killed white dove.
I am searching
for something I know
I've mislaid,

so I walk past comparsas of spices
with Spanish names
translated into English
feeling the urge
to dip one saliva-moistened finger into each pot
to savor the flavors,
hoping these tastes of
Cuba could help me

while my feet
shuffle down the aisles
remembering musical secretos,
keeping pace to the salsa songs
drifting from the transistor radio
which squats by the mounds of pennies
offered to San Lázaro

and I cha-cha-cha
imperceptibly
hypnotized by the sweet acrid scent
of café Cubano Bustelo
the old man below the cafeteria sign
pours with shaky hands
into tiny paper cups.

Hopeless

Laura Ymayo Tartakoff

They don't belong to me:
nor I to them—
neither London with her Westminster
and Christmas carols,
nor Cleveland with her blush-sky,
neither Geneva in her lake mirror
nor the whole of San Juan.

I know that in my birthplace Santiago,
which I don't remember,
it will be the same.

tr. from the Spanish by Lori M. Carlson

Irremediable

Laura Ymayo Tartakoff

No me pertenecen:
no les pertenezco—
ni Londres con su Westminster
y villancicos de Navidad,
ni Cleveland con su cielo rosa
ni Ginebra en su lago espejo
ni del todo San Juan.

Sé que en el Santiago natal
que no recuerdo,
lo mismo será.

Returning

Ruth Behar

I am going home.
I have the passport
with the four names
that once belonged to me
from the country we left

before I knew I had a country
before I knew I had no country.
Kuba, the promised land of jews
krazy to take a boat going anywhere
so long as it let them off in Amerika.

I cannot eat.
I am vomiting up my heart.
I am hearing the voices
of long-dead relatives.
My own life scares me.

I am going home.
Mami has told me
I may not come back.
Papi has told me
not to talk too much.

And there I am
again, in a small place
made huge by fear and forgetting
the way shadows haunt
when you won't look at them.

I see the two-bedroom apartment
where I would have grown up
as crowded as we did in New York.
I return to streets that don't
remember me, no matter how hard I step.

Regresando

Ruth Behar

Vuelvo a mi casa.
Llevo en el pasaporte
del país que abandonamos
los cuatro nombres
que una vez fueron míos

antes de saber que tenía un país
antes de saber que no tengo ningún país.
Kuba, la tierra prometida de los judíos
lokos por irse en bote a cualquier lado
mientras topasen con algún muelle de Amerika.

No puedo comer.
Me veo vomitar el corazón.
Oigo demasiadas voces
de parientes que hace tiempo murieron.
Me asusta mi propia vida.

Vuelvo a mi casa
Mami me dijo
que a lo mejor no voy a regresar.
Papi me dijo
que no hable demasiado.

Y de repente allí estoy
otra vez en ese pequeño lugar
hecho gigante por miedo y olvido
como las sombras que rondan
cuando no te atreves a mirarlas.

Veo el apartamento de dos cuartos
donde hubiera crecido
tan hacinados como en Nueva York.
Camino por calles que no quieren
recordarme aunque las pise bien fuerte.

tr. del inglés por la autora

We Are the Heirs

Rita Geada

We are the heirs.
The ones who build
fragile homes
in the storm.
The ones who open our tents
to unruly wind.
The ones who write deep words,
facing waves,
on the sand.

tr. from the Spanish by Lori M. Carlson

Somos los herederos

Rita Geada

Somos los herederos.
Los que construimos
frágiles moradas
bajo la tormenta.
Los que abrimos nuestras carpas
al ancho viento.
Los que escribimos hondas palabras,
frente a las olas,
sobre la arena.

The Photogenic Ones

Belkis Cuza Malé

Over the yellowed corners of a sheet of paper,
one can see them walk, disappear when the page is turned.
They inhabit an island in the tropics of war,
an island where all the glasses are broken,
an island on horseback.
They enter the suburbs of the afternoon
and transient hotels.
They navigate on a bed with white sails,
as he sings and she's just another sound,
a wave beneath the bed.
Better to be silent and let them sleep,
                and let them live
                and let them die.
At the bottom of the photo, a few lines
attest to the fact:
neither one is sure of the other,
but they navigate,
they navigate with the Island over all the seas of the world.

tr. from the Spanish by Daniel Shapiro

Los fotogénicos

Belkis Cuza Malé

Por las esquinas amarillentas de la hoja de papel
se les ve caminar, desaparecer al doblar la página.
Habitan una isla en el trópico de la guerra,
una isla donde todos los vasos están rotos,
una isla a caballo.
Entran en los suburbios de la tarde
y en los hoteles de paso,
navegan en una cama de velas blancas,
mientras él canta y ella es un ruido más,
una ola debajo de la cama.
Mejor callarse y dejarlos que duerman,
      y dejarlos que vivan,
      y dejarlos que mueran.
Al pie de la foto unas cuantas líneas
atestiguan el hecho:
ninguno está seguro del otro,
pero navegan,
navegan con la Isla por todos los mares del mundo.

For the Cuban Dead

Ricardo Pau-Llosa

Once they were men fully because they belonged,
and everywhere they looked and chatted and sipped
a bit of coffee, whisked away a fly with a wrist
or jolted a newspaper readably straight,
or flirted, or worried about the world and where
the damn country was going as a trolley rolled
and curtains dipped and bulged breast-like
and hid again in the proper window. They were
home and citizens of it and dared and loved
and were decent and stole and killed and loved again.
They were home. How like the root in the earth,
the crease in the linen, the wind rending the cloud,
the growl in the hunger, the pavement sprayed
with waves crashing against the sea wall.
How like all right things in the mind of place,
they jostled and failed, learned and betrayed.
Like coins in pockets made for them
they cried stridently or simply tinkled in murmurs,
and it didn't matter if talk or life had substance.
Right of place was substance.

There is no *enough* in exile. Not enough anger,
and the blanket of safety always leaves the feet bare.
And it is here, no matter how clean and golden,
that one learns how different the wrist and the fly
and the shot of wave, how it never stops
calling although the law of distance deafens.
Memory is the heart's gravity.
The accent of their children

becomes unbearably alien, a dampness
from the sidewalk creeping past the thin sole
and into the ignored sock. Now nothing
escapes notice and the balance is always against.

And it hits them, these never again composed,
that the time to see and hear was then,
when rightness held even the stormy evils
of the quotidian in the same palm
with the trash of years of seconds
and the kissed joys.
Then, as we have come to know, was
the proper place to gaze at the dust
of butterfly panoplies, ponder
the calligraphic crud on china,
relinquish decorous ears to taut goatskins,
wash in the lace of Sunday clouds,
and otherwise pay attention
with one's whole life to shadows
knitting five centuries of incomparable capital,
field's antique jewel, and the cradling shore.
God it was who let them die
filled with late understanding,
so who dares say we the innocent lurk
unpunished in the works and days?

Para los muertos cubanos

Ricardo Pau-Llosa

Alguna vez fueron hombres a plenitud porque pertenecían,
y dondequiera que miraran, conversaban, sorbían
buches de café, espantaban moscas con la mano,
o de golpe enderezaban un periódico para leerlo,
o coqueteaban, o se preocupaban sobre el estado
del mundo y por dónde iba el dichoso país,
mientras rodaban en tranvía y pasaban cortinas
que se hundían o brotaban como senos para volver
a esconderse dentro de la ventana sobria. Estaban
en casa y eran sus ciudadanos y se atrevían y amaban
y eran decentes y robaban y mataban y volvían a amar.
Estaban en casa. Cuánto se parecían a la raíz en tierra,
la arruga en el lino, el viento rasgando una nube,
el gruñir dentro del hambre, el pavimento cubierto
con olas estallando contra el malecón.
Eran como cualquier cosa propia situada
en la mente de un lugar, y empujaban y fracasaban,
aprendían y traicionaban. Como monedas
en bolsillos especialmente hechos para ellas,
chillaban o simplemente tintineaban en murmullos,
y no importaba si lo que se decía o vivía tenía sustancia.
El derecho a estar era sustancia.

No hay *basta* en el exilio. No hay suficiente ira,
y la colcha de la seguridad siempre deja los pies afuera.
Y es aquí, no importa cuán limpio o dorado,
que uno aprende cuán diferente eran la mano y la mosca
y el disparo de la ola, como *entonces* nunca para
de llamar aunque la ley de la distancia ensordece.

La memoria es la gravedad del corazón.
El acento de sus hijos se hace insoportablemente
foráneo, una humedad que desde la acera
se cuela por la suela más fina y se prende
de la media ignorada. Ahora nada escapa
la perspicacia y el saldo es siempre en contra.

Y les viene de golpe, a estos seres que jamás
volverán a estar compuestos, que el tiempo de ver
y escuchar fue entonces, cuando la certeza apretaba
hasta los males borrascosos de cada día
en la misma palma con la basura de años de segundos
y las alegrías besadas. *Entonces,* como hemos llegado
a comprender, fue el lugar propio para contemplar el polvo
de panoplias de mariposas, ponderar el churre
caligráfico en el plato de porcelana,
entregar los oídos decorosos a los cueros de chivo,
lavarse en el encaje de los domingos,
y de cualquier forma prestar atención
con toda la presión de una vida a sombras
tejiendo cinco siglos de capital incomparable,
la joya antigua de los campos, y la cuna de la costa.
Fue Dios quien los dejó morirse
llenos de entendimiento tardío.
Entonces ¿quién se atreve a decir que nosotros,
los inocentes, nos movemos a escondidas
impunes en los trabajos y los días?

tr. del inglés por el autor

Destinies

Jesús J. Barquet

never dare say green lizard
—Luis Palés Matos

1. (Green Lizard)
My country? That curious in the water
green lizard that appears tenacious on video screens
in the planes I travel
between North America and South America,
and that I traverse in air always
above some city prone to errata:
Camagüey, Mariel, Matanzas, Cárdenas,
La Habana;
                 cities that could
—I imagine—
give me occasional refuge
in case of exhaustion or a breakdown
that might impede my arrival,
as I am accustomed,
in safety to my destiny.

2. (Exile)
Exile
is finally understanding
that the day we have awaited so long
will be nothing more than the news
between two commercials
for Pepsi and Tylenol.

tr. from the Spanish by Lori M. Carlson

Destinos

Jesús J. Barquet

jamás oséis decir lagarto verde
—Luis Palés Matos

1. (Lagarto verde)
¿Mi patria? Ese curioso entre las aguas
lagarto verde que aparece tenaz en las pantallas
de video de los aviones en que viajo
entre el Norte y el Sur americanos,
y que atravieso siempre desde el aire
por alguna ciudad adepta a las erratas:
Camagüey, Mariel, Matanzas, Cárdenas,
La Habana;
                        ciudades que podrían
—imagino—
darme refugio ocasional
en caso de cansancio o avería
que me impide llegar,
como acostumbro,
a salvo a mi destino.

2. (Exilio)
Exilio
es llegar a entender
que el día que tanto esperamos
no será más que una noticia
encapsulada entre dos comerciales
de Pepsi y Tylenol.

I Was Created in Silence

José Kozer

I was created in silence like a necessary complaint,
while they glanced at their watches as they fornicated.
Nothing more remote.
Nothing more beyond repair.
The fields withered, the old women conceived by the calendar,
the stars crashed down in the mud.
I was raised in a house without goldfish or music,
in the unending thread of inquisitions,
and only trees submerged in images provided shade.
I came of age systematically,
like an echo, a plant, like asphalt,
like the ancient prophet under a sky full of masks.

tr. from the Spanish by David Unger

Yo fui engendrado en silencio

José Kozer

Yo fui engendrado en silencio como una queja necesaria,
y mientras fornicaban consultaban los relojes.
Nada más distante.
Nada más irreparable.
Los campos se secaron, las viejas concibieron por el calendario,
se fueron desprendiendo las estrellas en el fango.
Yo crecí en una casa sin peces y sin música,
yo crecí en la hilera continua de las inquisiciones,
y sólo sombra los árboles sumidos en imágenes.
Yo vine a madurar, sistemáticamente,
como el eco, como la planta, como el asfalto,
como el profeta antiguo con el cielo poblado de máscaras.

Man Conceived

Lourdes Gil

There is a humid order making its premiere in clay
an echo in adobe scent
a vastness inhabited by sound
a buzzing in the cortex

Language, alive, goes scheming in earth
stiletto thought
the erect idea in synovial matter
(ah, incense)
membrane of bean, pelisse of certainty.

tr. from the Spanish by Lori M. Carlson

Concebido el hombre

Lourdes Gil

Hay un húmedo orden estrenándose en el barro
un eco de adobe en el olfato
una vastedad poblada de sonidos
un zumbido en la corteza.

El lenguaje, vivo, va urdiéndose en la arcilla
el pensamiento de *stiletto*
la idea erguida en la materia sinovial
(ah, incienso)
membrana del frijol, pelliza de lo cierto.

The Island

Pura del Prado

for my children, René and Raúl Pedraza

The Island will forever be invincibly alive,
though we be missing.
She will survive historical ruins,
her emigrations
and political conflicts.
It is good thus.
It comforts one to know as the centuries pass
her soil will be there always roiling foam
under the nimbus of mandarin aureoles,
with her inviolable green,
the fingers of her palms scratching
the chords of wind when it rains.
And may her name be always: Cuba!
her sun steadfast
and may she always be accompanied
by the hymns and harvests of men.
When all her cities lay beneath the dust,
when her generations disappear
after her cataclysms,
my cyclonic mother will float among the waves,
delicate and unscathed,
a crystalline amoeba.
I am glad she can forgo her statues and lighthouses,
governments and wars,
the follies of her inhabitants.
I am happy knowing God watches her for me

with His eternal sweetness,
an archer astride the horizon of hope.
Maybe, maybe one day
we will see her from a flight of angels,
a prodigious emerald
adrift upon the all-embracing song of the sea.
Splendid and open
this woman shining toward the dawn.

tr. from the Spanish by the author and René Pedraza

La Isla

Pura del Prado

para mis hijos, René y Raúl Pedraza

La Isla estará siempre invictamente viva,
aunque faltemos.
Sobrevivirá a los derrumbes históricos,
las emigraciones
y los conflictos políticos.
Es bueno que así sea.
Consuela pensar que al paso de los siglos
la tierra estará allí chorreando espumas,
bajo los nimbos de orlas mandarinas,
con su verde inviolable,
los dedos de sus palmas arañando
el cordaje del viento cuando llueve.
Y ojalá que se llame siempre Cuba,
que el sol no me la olvide,
que la acompañen himnos y renuevos del hombre.
Cuando las ciudades estén bajo el polvo,
cuando las generaciones desaparezcan
después de los cataclismos,
mi ciclónica madre flotará entre las aguas,
delicada e indemne,
con sustancia de ameba cristalina.
Me alegro que pueda prescindir de las estatuas y los faros,
los gobiernos y las guerras,
las locuras del habitante.
Soy feliz comprendiendo como Dios me la cuida
con la eternidad de su dulzura,

arquero en su horizonte de esperanza.
Quizá, quizá algún día
la veremos desde un vuelo de ángeles,
como a esmeralda pródiga
sobre la canción omnímoda del mar.
Espléndida y abierta
esta mujer que alumbra hacia la mañana.

Words Are Islands

Orlando González Esteva

Words are islands
fabulous, disperse
in the sea of silence.
Only the caravels

of death devour
the distance between them.
We don't write: we set sail
upon the blank page

toward the unknown.
A poem is the wake.

tr. from the Spanish by Lori M. Carlson

Las palabras son islas

Orlando González Esteva

      Las palabras son islas
fabulosas, dispersas
en el mar del silencio.
Sólo las carabelas

      de la muerte devoran
la distancia entre ellas.
No escribimos: zarpamos
por la página abierta

      a lo desconocido.
El poema es la estela.

If You Press Me

Uva de Aragón

If you press me
if you force me
if you come to take me from my timorous silence
I will tell you few things matter
although those few things multiply
like an echo of endless possibilities.
I will think about the sun, the light, the fire.
I will think about the rain, the sea, the rivers.
I will speak of the wind, the breeze, the storms.
I will tell you about the earth, the seed, the trees.
About man, death, hope.
I will look into your eyes. And I will tell you it's enough.

tr. from the Spanish by Lori M. Carlson

Si me precisas

Uva de Aragón

Si me precisas
si me obligas
si vienes a sacarme de mi tímido silencio
te diré que sólo hay algunas pocas cosas
aunque esas mismas cosas se multipliquen
como un eco de posibilidades infinitas.
Pensaré en el sol, la luz, el fuego.
Pensaré en la lluvia, el mar, los ríos.
Te hablaré del aire, la brisa, la tormenta.
Te contaré sobre la tierra, la espiga, el árbol.
Sobre el hombre, la muerte y la esperanza.
Me miraré en tus ojos. Y te diré que basta.

To the Rumba Players of Belén, Cuba
...An Interpretation of a Song...

Adrián Castro

Those drums are committed
are relics
for & de that space
where rumba had its crib.
Legacy of aboriginal cane cutters
traders in spice
the deathly odor
of salted meats.
Sweat sí & yes
that humidity
that humidity ruffled by the sun.

Bongó conga clave
cajón
these are breathing
museums of two cultures
these are the autochthonous
of tone
of rhythm
of speech.

That man leaning on a corner
that woman undulating in a river
that child standing at
a crossroad with
a steel crown
they have not forgotten

the echo of the batá
chiseled into cement
sculptures of hooded monks.
Cobblestone roads hot
as July asphalt
bien caliente because today
September 8th
today tumbadoras are fondled
for La Caridad del Cobre
known around Belén
as Ochún.

Those festivals in plazas presided
by the king Chano Pozo
his fingers aflame
slurrin' hymns in Lucumí
Abakuá
Lucumí Arará
raspy rum rails.
Negras with long yellow
skirts copper bracelets
dancing a sensual shake
twinkling their eyes
in a heavy African ogle
cooling honeydew drops
with fans of peacock feather.

Chickens & roosters walking their struts
oblivious to their sacred blood.
Church and jungle symbolized
Seville and Ile Ifé ritualized.
Those rumberos will not
forget the marriage arranged
on high seas.

A new identity writ
in ominous swells. A new
breed of troubadour.
Esas negras will continue
the snapping sway of hips
the tremble of thighs
to the crisp leather
crackling wood
their union
bonded by fingers aflame
responding to burning tongues.

Imagine the first tún-tún!
Did Chano Pozo inherit
he whose ears were present
at the first drumming?
Astonishing the first callus!
Oye Chano
are your hands homesick
when not beating on goatskins?
Sobering the first sting of rum!
There are some
who say they saw
his birth in Belén.
Some say he wore colored collares/
necklaces so his congas
could commune with deities.
Some even say he baptized rumberos
with rum.

Oye Chano Pozo
did you have calluses
the size of coconuts?

Did you
wear collares
when you breathed your
last sigh?

Elegía de María Belén Chacón

Emilio Ballagas

María Belén, María Belén, María Belén.
María Belén Chacón, María Belén Chacón, María Belén
        Chacón,
con tus nalgas en vaivén,
de Camagüey a Santiago, de Santiago a Camagüey.

En el cielo de la rumba,
ya nunca habrá de alumbrar
tu constelación de curvas.

¿Qué ladrido te mordió el vértice del pulmón?
María Belén Chacón, María Belén Chacón...
¿Qué ladrido te mordió el vértice del pulmón?

Ni fue ladrido ni uña,
ni fue uña ni fue *daño*.
¡La plancha, de madrugada, fue quien te quemó el pulmón!
María Belén Chacón, María Belén Chacón...

Y luego, por la mañana,
con la ropa, en la canasta, se llevaron tu sandunga
tu sandunga y tu pulmón.

¡Que no baile nadie ahora!
¡Que no le arranque más pulgas el negro Andrés
a su tres!

Y los chinos, que arman tanganas adentro de las maracas,
hagan un poco de paz.

Besar la cruz de las claves.
(¡Líbranos de todo mal, Virgen de la Caridá!)

Ya no veré mis instintos
en los espejos redondos y alegres de tus dos nalgas.
Tu constelación de curvas
ya no alumbrará jamás el cielo de la sandunga.

María Belén Chacón, María Belén Chacón.
María Belén, María Belén:
con tus nalgas en vaivén,
de Camagüey a Santiago...,
de Santiago a Camagüey.

Going Bananas

Rita María Martínez

My father rises each morning
to the seventeen varieties of banana trees
he's cultivated with unrivaled
care, each tree casting shade across our lawn,
each racimo an offering my father hacks
with his machete, a small cruelty
he performs like a doctor circumcising
a newborn, though I like to think
he is unburdening these trees,
casting weight off the tired trunks
of his Aromatic; his Honduran Goldfinger
and its hybrids (Fhia-3 and Fhia-18);
his twenty-two-foot-tall Saba,
tallest banana tree in the world;
his Mona Lisa, Lady's Finger, Ice Cream banana;
his Apple Sugar, a.k.a. Mansano;
his plátano Enano: Dwarf Cavendish,
sweet midget sacrificed
to the blender for smoothies;
his Jamaican Red, his Cuban Red;
his Misi Luki; his Mysore; his 3640;
his Gran Nain; and my favorite, Orinoco—
plátano Burro he hauls into the house
with the pride of a hunter.
When he enters the kitchen wearing
his sweat-stained *Going Bananas* T-shirt
my mother stares at the shoot
dangling from his hands
like a third arm and smiles,

though I know she's thinking
of resin that'll cling to the cutting board
and her fingers, but he submits los plátanos
like a boy bringing a drawing
to be exhibited on the refrigerator door,
so she strips, slices, mashes, fries
until they're crunchy, sweet and salted
tostones, mini-sunflowers humbly
acquiescing beside the breaded steak
on my father's ivory dinner plate.

Going Bananas

Rita María Martínez

Mi papá se levanta cada mañana
a saludar las diecisiete variedades
de árboles de plátano que ha cultivado
con cuidado incomparable, cada árbol que lanza
sombra a través de nuestro césped,
cada racimo una ofrenda mi papa desprende
con su machete, una pequeña crueldad
que realiza como un médico que circuncida
a un recién nacido. Aunque yo pienso
que está librando estas matas cansadas,
aliviando el peso de los troncos fatigados
de Aromático; su Goldfinger Hondureño
y sus híbridos (Fhia-3 y Fhia-18);
de su Saba, que mide veinte-dos-pies—
la variedad más alta en el mundo,
su Mona Lisa, Dedo de Dama, Ice Cream Banana;
su Mansano (Apple Sugar);
su plátano Enano: Dwarf Cavendish,
pequeñitos sacrificados a la licuadora;
su Rojo Jamaiquino, su Rojo Cubano;
su Misi Luki; su Mysore; su 3640;
su Gran Nain; y mi favorito, Orinoco—
plátano Burro que acarrea en la casa con el orgullo
de un casador. Cuando él entra la cocina,
su *Going Bananas* camisa está empapada
de sudor y mamá observa el racimo
colgando de sus manos como un tercer braso
y sonríe, aunque yo sé que ella
está pensando en resina que se pegará

a la plancha para cortar y a sus dedos,
pero él entrega los plátanos como
un chico somete un dibjuo escolar
para ser exhibido en la puerta del refrigerador.
Así que ella corta, pela, aplasta, fríe
hasta que los tostones son dulces
y salados, hasta que lucen como girasoles
asintiendo humildemente al lado
del bistec empanizado en el plato de marfil.

tr. del inglés por la autora

The Gardener

Carolina Hospital

I sit on the crisp grass
and slowly pull the weeds
around the newly planted
Manila palms and purple heather.
The dirt sneaks
into the creases in my skin.
I avoid the sun rays dappling the ground.
A gray covers the skies.
I let the scent of the warm soil,
the humidity in the air,
the stillness before the summer shower
transport me north
to the mountain forest,
of rhododendrons and spruce pine,
south to la finca,
with its cafetales and sugarcane fields.
For an instant, I exist in three spaces.
Back in my garden, I look around.
I realize it doesn't matter.
The hibiscus and bougainvilleas
I have planted
are blooming.
In any soil,
they are the same,
as long as they grow
nourished and unfettered.

La jardinera

Carolina Hospital

Me siento sobre la hierba mojada.
Una a una arranco las malas
en torno a la palma y el brezo morado
acabados de sembrar.
Entre los pliegues de mi piel
se esconde la tierra.
El cielo se cubre de gris.
Evito los rayos del sol moteando el suelo.
Dejo que aquel olor a tierra en llamas,
la humedad,
el silencio que anticipa la lluvia
me trasladen
al norte
a los bosques
de rododendros y abetos
al sur
a la finca
con sus cafetales y cañaverales.
Existo, por un instante,
en tres espacios.
Ya en mi jardín, lo reconozco.
No importa.
Los marpacíficos y buganvilias
que he sembrado
han florecido.
En cualquier suelo
serán los mismos
si crecen
sin ataduras.

tr. del inglés por la autora

Years of Discourse

Dionisio D. Martínez

are not always preceded by years of silence. More than likely, they follow unfulfilled demands.

An arsenal of threats is dismantled.

The hands of the adversary begin to look surprisingly lifelike.

For the agnostics, a man with cancer in his throat heals himself and begins to sing like a broken angel.

Those most susceptible to nostalgia are reminded of the mythical Age of Miracles.

An arsenal of memories, long abandoned, is discovered and restored.

Familiar voices reappear. In proportion to the sky, they are whispers.

Los años de conversación

Dionisio D. Martínez

no siempre son precedidos por años de silencio.
Más probable es que sigan exigencias incumplidas.

Se desmantela un arsenal de amenazas.

Las manos del adversario comienzan a parecer
sorprendentemente humanas.

Para el agnóstico el canceroso de la garganta
se cura solo y comienza a cantar como ángel quebrantado.

Los extremadamente susceptibles a la nostalgia recuerdan
la mítica Edad de los Milagros.

Un arsenal de memorias por largo tiempo abandonado
queda descubierto y restaurado.

Conocidas voces resurgen; en proporción al cielo,
son susurros

tr. del inglés por Warren Hampton

With Bare Hands

Dolores Prida

to G. A. Becquer

I, with bare hands
want to build a temple
so that
I can play
the harp
so that
I can sing
a hymn
to raise the dead.

I, with ravaged voice
want to revive poetry
so that
ears
hear
so that
hearts
beat
to go on
living.

tr. from the Spanish by Lori M. Carlson

Con las manos desnudas

Dolores Prida

a G. A. Becquer

Yo, con las manos desnudas
quiero construir un templo
para
tocar
el arpa
para
cantar
un himno
para
levantar los muertos.

Yo, con la voz desgarrada
quiero revivir la poesía
para que
los oídos
escuchen
para que
los corazones
latan
para seguir
viviendo.

Bebita I

Armando Valladares

Your name is a blue
leaf of time
the end point
of the universe
a dream of pulverized
crystal
in my hands
of lover becoming verse

tr. from the Spanish by Lori M. Carlson

Bebita I

Armando Valladares

Tu nombre es una hoja
azul de tiempo
un punto final del Universo
un sueño de cristal
pulverizado
que en mis manos
de amante se hace verso.

Acknowledgments

The editors are deeply grateful to the following: Bob Weil, Victor and Virginia Cruz, Martha Levin, Amy Scheibe, Maris Kreizman, Jennifer Lyons, and all of the poets and heirs of the poets who contributed to this collection.

Acknowledgements

Contributors

José Abreu Felippe was born in La Habana in 1947. He left Cuba in 1983 and has lived in exile in Miami since 1987. A writer of plays, he has also written the novels *Siempre la lluvia* and *Dile adiós a la virgen*. His two books of poetry are *Orestes de noche* and *Cantos y elegías*.

Agustín Acosta was born in Matanzas, Cuba, in 1886, and came to the United States in 1972. In 1955 he was named National Poet of Cuba. A writer of essays, articles, letters, and poems, among his published books are *Ala, El Apóstol y su isla, La Zafra, Las islas desoladas, Caminos de hierro,* and *Trigo de luna.* He died in Miami in 1979.

Uva de Aragón was born in La Habana in 1944, and is a poet as well as a journalist. She now lives in Miami. A professor at Florida International University, she is associate director of the Cuban Research Institute. Among her published books are *Eternidad, Versos de exilio,* and *Entresemáforos (poemas escritos en ruta).*

Reinaldo Arenas was born in Holguín, Cuba, and left Cuba during the Mariel boat lift in 1980. In the United States he cofounded and edited the cultural magazine *Mariel.* A novelist, poet, and memoirist, among his published books are *Singing from the Well, The Palace of the White Skunks,* and *Before Night Falls.* He died in 1990 in New York City.

EMILIO BALLAGAS was born in Cuba in 1908. Known for its inventive and experimental poetry, in which Ballagas attempted to make meaning of word-sound, his work was outstanding within the "negrista" framework. Among his published works are *Cuaderno de poesía negra, Sabor eterno,* and *Nuestra señora del mar.* He died in Cuba in 1954.

JESÚS J. BARQUET was born in La Habana in 1953. He arrived in the United States during the Mariel boat lift in 1980. Since 1991 he has been a professor at New Mexico State University in Las Cruces. In addition to writing poetry he is an editor and translator. Among his books of poetry are *Un no rompido sueño, Sin fecha de extinción,* and *Naufragios.*

RUTH BEHAR is professor of anthropology at the University of Michigan. She is the author of *Translated Woman: Crossing the Border with Esperanza's Story,* which brought her national prominence, and the editor of *Bridges to Cuba,* among many other publications.

LUIS CARTAÑÁ was born in La Habana in 1942. He received his law degree from La Universidad Complutense de Madrid and taught literature at the University of Puerto Rico in Mayagüez. He died in Miami in 1989. Among his published books are *Estos humanos dioses, La joven resina, Sobre la música,* and *La mandarina y el fuego.*

WALTER DE LAS CASAS was born in La Habana in 1947, and has lived in the United States since 1960. His poetry has appeared in many literary journals, including *Linden Lane Magazine.* Among his books of poetry is *La niñez que dilata.*

SANDRA M. CASTILLO is a poet and essayist. She was born in La Habana and moved to the United States in 1970. Among her published books are *Red Letters; My Father Sings, to My Embarrassment;* and *Last Night in Havana.*

ADRIÁN CASTRO was born in Miami in 1967 to Cuban and Dominican parents. A poet who often recites his work to live music, he has published *Cantos to Blood & Honey.* His work has appeared in *Paper Dance: 55 Latino Poets, Little Havana Blues,* and *The Miami Herald,* among other publications.

RAFAEL CATALÁ was born in Victoria de las Tunas in 1942. He completed all of his university studies in New York City at New York University and now lives in St. Petersburg, Florida. Among his published books are *Caminos/Roads, Círculo cuadrado, Copulantes,* and *Cienciapoesía.*

ANGEL CUADRA was born in La Habana in 1931. He graduated from the University of Havana's law school and practiced law until 1967, when he became a political prisoner in Cuba for fifteen years. Since 1985 he has lived in exile in Miami, where he has taught at various universities, including Florida International University. Among his many books are *La voz inevitable, Diez sonetos ocultos,* and *De los resúmenes y el tiempo.*

BELKIS CUZA MALÉ was born in Guantánamo. A poet, essayist, and biographer, she moved to the United States with her late husband, Heberto Padilla, in 1979. She edits the literary magazine *Linden Lane.* Among her published books are *El clavel y la rosa, Woman on the Front Lines,* and *Tiempo del sol.*

EUGENIO FLORIT, whose mother was Cuban, was born in Madrid in 1903, and completed his secondary and university studies in La Habana. One of Cuba's most influential poets and essayists, he lived at various times in Spain, Cuba, and the United States. Among his published books are *Trópico, Donde habite el recuerdo,* and *Momentos.* He died in Miami in 1999.

RITA GEADA was born in Pinar del Río, Cuba, in 1937. She left in 1961, going first to Argentina for postgraduate studies before coming to the United States, where she has taught literature at Southern Connecticut State University in New Haven, Connecticut. Currently she lives in Miami Beach. Among her books are *Mascarada, Cuando cantan las pisadas, Esa lluvia de fuego que nos quema, Espejo de tierra,* and *El mar sigue batiendo.*

LOURDES GIL was born in La Habana in 1950. Since 1961 she has lived in the United States and currently teaches in the Department of Latin American and Caribbean Studies at Baruch College. She is a translator and cultural critic, as well as a poet, and her published work includes *El cerco de las transfiguraciones, Blanca aldaba preludia,* and *Empieza la ciudad.*

ORLANDO GONZÁLEZ ESTEVA was born in Santiago de Cuba in 1952. He studied at Washington University, where he received his M.A. in Hispanic literature, and taught literature in Miami from 1976 to 1980. A playwright and poet, his books include *El ángel perplejo, El mundo se dilata,* and *El pájaro tras la flecha.*

CAROLINA HOSPITAL is a Cuban-American poet, essayist, and fiction writer who lives and teaches in Miami. Her poetry has appeared in numerous anthologies and publications, among them *The Washington Post, Prairie Schooner,* and *Confrontation.* She has also authored *Cuban American Writers: Los atrevidos.*

FAYAD JAMÍS was born in 1930 in Zacatecas, Mexico, and came to Cuba with his family in 1949. Among his published books of poetry are *La pedrada, Brújula, Los párpados y el polvo,* and *Abrí la verja de hierro.* He died in Cuba in 1988.

JOSÉ KOZER was born in La Habana in 1940. He left in 1960 and lived in New York until 1997, where he taught in the Department of Romance Languages at Queens College in New York. He now lives in Florida. Among his books are *Padres y otras profesiones, Poemas de Guadalupe, The Ark Upon the Number,* and *De donde oscilan los seres en sus proporciones.*

DIONISIO D. MARTÍNEZ was born in La Habana in 1956. In 1965 he and his family left Cuba for Spain. He currently lives in Florida. Among his published books of poetry are *History as a Second Language, Bad Alchemy,* and *Climbing Back.*

RITA MARÍA MARTÍNEZ is a native Floridian who lives in Fort Lauderdale. Her poetry has appeared in numerous publications—including *Ploughshares, Mangrove,* and *Gargoyle*—and is included in the forthcoming books *Three Genres: The Editing of Poetry, Fiction and Drama,* and *Saints of Hysteria.* She has taught at Miami Dade College.

PABLO MEDINA, a poet, translator, and novelist, was born in La Habana and has lived in the United States since 1960. Among his published books are *Pork Rind and Cuban Songs, Arching into the Afterlife, Exiled Memories: A Cuban Childhood, The Marks of Birth,* and *The Cigar Roller.*

LISSETTE MÉNDEZ was born in La Habana and came to the United States in the Mariel boat lift in 1980. A program coordinator at the Florida Center for Literary Arts at Miami Dade

College, she writes nonfiction and poetry. Her poetry has been published in anthologies and literary journals, including *Blue Mesa Review*, *TriQuarterly*, *Kalliope*, and *Rattle*.

ACHY OBEJAS, born in La Habana in 1956, is a poet, journalist, and fiction writer who lives in Chicago. Among her published books are *Days of Awe*; *Memory Mambo*; *Salao, or the Worst Form of Unlucky*; and *We Came All the Way from Cuba So You Could Dress Like This?*

HEBERTO PADILLA, one of Cuba's best-known writers, was born in 1932 in Pinar del Río. A poet, novelist, and journalist, he was arrested and imprisoned briefly in 1971 because of a book of poems critical of the government—an episode commonly referred to as "El caso Padilla." In 1980 he was permitted to leave the country, whereupon he came to the United States. Among his published books are *Legacies: Selected Poems*, *El justo tiempo humano*, *Heroes Are Grazing in My Garden*, and *Fuera del juego*. He died in Alabama in 2000.

RICARDO PAU-LLOSA was born in La Habana in 1954, and has lived in Florida since 1960. He is the author of six poetry collections, of which the last four are published by Carnegie Mellon: *Cuba*, *Vereda Tropical*, *The Mastery Impulse*, and the forthcoming *Parable Hunter*. He is also an art critic specializing in twentieth-century Latin American painting and sculpture.

GUSTAVO PÉREZ FIRMAT is a poet, essayist, and literary critic. He was born in 1949 in La Habana, and was raised in Miami. He teaches in the Spanish department of Duke University. Among his published books are *Life on the Hyphen*, *Bilingual Blues*, and *Next Year in Cuba*.

PURA DEL PRADO, born in 1931 in Santiago, Cuba, was a poet, teacher, actress, and journalist. Beginning in 1958, she lived first in Europe and then in the United States. Among her published books are *De todos en el arco iris, La otra orilla,* and *Canto a Martí.* She died in Miami in 1996.

DOLORES PRIDA was born in Caibarién, Cuba, in 1943, and has lived in New York since 1961. A journalist, short story writer, poet, and playwright, she is perhaps best known for her plays, among them *Beautiful Señoritas and Other Plays* and *Coser y cantar.* Among her published poetry volumes is *Treinta y un poemas.*

ORLANDO ROSSARDI was born in La Habana in 1938. In 1960 he left Cuba for Spain, then came to the United States, where he has taught at several universities. An essayist, playwright, short story writer, and poet, he has written volumes of poetry including *El diámetro y lo estero, Que voy de vuelo, Los espacios llenos,* and *Memoria de mí.* He currently lives in Doral, Florida.

ENRIQUE SACERIO-GARÍ was born in Sagua la Grande, Cuba, in 1945. A professor in the Spanish department of Bryn Mawr College, he has contributed poems to anthologies and magazines in the United States, Spain, and Cuba. He is the author of the poetry collection *Poemas interreales.*

SEVERO SARDUY was born in Camagüey in 1937. He moved to Paris in 1960. A journalist, novelist, poet, and literary and art critic, his published works include *De dónde son los cantantes, Escrito sobre un cuerpo, Barroco,* and *Un testigo fugaz y dizfrazado; un testigo perenne y delatado.* He died in Paris in 1993.

VIRGIL SUÁREZ, born in La Habana in 1962, is a poet, editor, and novelist. In 1970 he moved to Spain, where he lived for four years; now he resides in Tallahassee, Florida. Among his published books are *Welcome to the Oasis, Garabato Poems, In the Republic of Longing,* and *Iguana Dreams,* as well as four novels, including *Havana Thursdays* and *Latin Jazz.*

LAURA YMAYO TARTAKOFF was born in Santiago, Cuba, in 1954, and currently teaches in the Department of Political Science at Case Western Reserve University in Cleveland, Ohio. Her interests center around poetry, democratization, and human rights. Among her books of poetry are *Mujer martes, Entero lugar* and *Intimo color.*

ARMANDO VALLADARES was born in Pinar del Río in 1937. For twenty-two years he was a political prisoner in La Habana. Upon his release in 1981 he left the country for Madrid, Spain. He now lives in Miami, Florida. Among his published books are *Desde mi silla de ruedas, El corazón con que vivo, Cavernas del silencio,* and *Contra toda esperanza.*

Editors

LORI MARIE CARLSON holds an M.A. in Hispanic literature from Indiana University and is a former director of literature at the Americas Society in New York City. An editor, translator, and novelist, her books include *The Sunday Tertulia* and the Landmark Award–winning poetry anthology *Cool Salsa: Bilingual Poems on Growing Up Latino in the United States.*

OSCAR HIJUELOS holds an M.F.A. in creative writing from the City College of New York. A Cuban-American, he is the first Latino to have won the Pulitzer Prize in fiction, for his novel *The Mambo Kings Play Songs of Love.* His six other novels include the acclaimed *Mr. Ives' Christmas.* His work has been translated into thirty-five languages.

Permission Acknowledgments

"The Rain." Copyright © Gustavo Pérez Firmat. Reprinted by his permission.

"Rain." Copyright © José Abreu Felippe. Reprinted by his permission.

"1898 Vistas." Copyright © Enrique Sacerio-Garí. Reprinted by his permission.

"Autumn Presents Me with a Leaf." Copyright © Reinaldo Arenas. Reprinted by permission of Lázaro Gómez.

"I Have Always Lived in Cuba." Copyright © Heberto Padilla. Reprinted by permission of Belkis Cuza Malé.

"A Poem for the Epiphany." Copyright © Pablo Medina. Reprinted by his permission.

"I've Never Seen It Snow." Copyright © Agustín Acosta. Reprinted by permission of Sara Orbon.

"From Head to Toe." Copyright © Luis Cartañá. Reprinted by permission of Betania Ediciones, Madrid.

"Feet." Copyright © Rafael Catalá. Reprinted by his permission.

"Loving You Is a Way of Being." Copyright © Angel Cuadra. Reprinted by his permission.

"Memories." Copyright © Eugenio Florit. Reprinted by permission of Ricardo Florit.

"Weariness." Copyright © Orlando Rossardi. Reprinted by his permission.

"To José Martí." Copyright © Walter de las Casas. Reprinted by his permission.